Anne
BOLEYN

WHO WAS...

Anne
BOLEYN

The Queen who lost her head

LAURA BEATTY

✳ **SHORT BOOKS**

Published in 2004 by

Short Books

15 Highbury Terrace

London N5 1UP

10 9 8 7 6 5 4 3 2

A CIP catalogue record for this book
is available from the British Library.

ISBN 1-904095-78-X

Printed in Great Britain by
Bookmarque Ltd, Croydon, Surrey

CHAPTER ONE

Across the watery wilds of Norfolk rumbles a dark carriage. Inside is little Anne Boleyn, 12 years old, setting out on a long and uncertain journey to a foreign court. It is 1513. Behind her, still in darkness, is Blickling Castle, where she was born. Ahead of her is Dover and the dawn.

At Dover, Anne takes a boat for France. If she is lucky and the wind is fair, the journey will take two or three hours. If it is stormy it might take a day. She has none of her family with her. No one to comfort her when she cries on the rocking ship that takes her away from her homeland. No one to help her if she is seasick, if she slips on the wooden deck in her long skirts. No one to reassure her, if she is frightened of the wild-faced sailors running in the rigging, with their earrings and their bare feet.

Anne's only travelling companion is a man she has never met before, Claude Bouton, Seigneur de Courbaron of Flanders. He is taking her to the palace of Mechelen to be one of the 18 maids of honour at the Habsburg Court – to learn to be a lady, to dance, to dress, to speak French. If she is homesick, she can write a letter but she must wait until someone is going to England and can take it for her. There is no postal service. A reply might take two weeks to a month to come. She does not know it now, but it is nine years before Anne will go home again.

***

The Boleyns of Blickling – the family that Anne left behind her – were grand enough but they were not rich. Her father's ambition was to make them both. He wanted money and he wanted land and he was not above using his children to get it. There were three of them, Mary, George and Anne. We do not know what Anne thought of her elder sister, but she was fond of her brother. No one liked Thomas, her father, who was 'mean and grasping' and 'not beloved'.

Thomas Boleyn, the unbeloved, was a courtier. If you wanted to advance yourself in Tudor times there were two main ways to go about it. You could enter the church and become a priest, or you could go to Court. Either way you needed to get close to the King. There was no elected government like there is now, no politicians or Prime Minister. One person chose what rules were made and that person was the King. If you could attract his attention, if you could gain his friendship and his good opinion, then the sky was the limit.

Court was a bog of self-interest, a quick-sand of flatterers and back-stabbers, of false friends and hidden enemies. No one cared about anyone else. Everyone scrambled and elbowed and pushed and shoved to get into the charmed circle around the King. It was the perfect place for Thomas Boleyn.

All three little Boleyns were bred to be courtiers,

like their father. They were brought up to mistrust their friends, to be shrewd, manipulative, fearless, risk-taking and wary as a fox. Then they were sent off, told to make powerful allies, to look for money – the girls in particular. They were the family's best chance. If they were clever they would snare a rich man into marriage. That was their duty. That was what Thomas hoped.

Anne had plenty of time – two years at Mechelen and seven more in France, as lady-in-waiting to Queen Claude, the ugly little 15-year-old wife of Frances I. She spent her years watching the world. She was clever. She saw that women had no will of their own, that they were bargained over like groceries; bought and sold by the men who owned them – fathers, brothers, uncles, husbands.

At last, a message came to Anne from her father. If she married the Earl of Ormonde, the Boleyns would get their hands on some more property. She must come back at once. So Anne set out again, this time for a difficult winter crossing, and with nine years experience behind her. She arrived in time to have her unknown husband described to her and to help with the wedding preparations. Did she want to marry? Did she want to live in Ireland? No one asked.

CHAPTER TWO

What was it like, the England that Anne came home to? – a wild and muddy place; a boastful country, always up for a fight, but compared to the Europe Anne knew, a country that was small and backward. Travel was difficult. There were robbers and cut-throats and forests full of wolves. Communications did not exist. News came as fast as a horse could gallop, by word of mouth or by written message. Life was short. If you were ill, doctors stuck leeches to your body to suck your blood, or made you potions out of flour and ground caterpillars. Most children died before they were ten. If you grew up you could expect to live to about 40.

But it was a good place to live if you were brave

and had your wits about you. Ships were being built, and schools, and churches. Books were being written, maps drawn, rules made, new thoughts thought. Everywhere, everything growing, changing, bursting with the energy of men who were not afraid, men who would risk their lives to make their fortune – explorers, adventurers, tricksters, pirates, musicians, writers – and women, women like Anne Boleyn, who were cunning and ambitious and fearless and out to make their mark, just like the men.

The king of this country was Henry the Eighth, and his queen, fat, holy and Spanish, was Katherine of Aragon. They were very different. Katherine was six years older than him and it was beginning to show. She was interested in God and the poor. Henry was interested in spending money, in music, in jousting and dancing, in clever men and pretty women, but most of all he was interested in his kingdom and who would inherit it when he was gone. He had no son to follow him and that was a problem, a serious problem.

Henry's problem lay in the back of his mind and

worked like a rat at his confidence. It worried him as he went about England hunting and feasting. It worried him in the night if he woke with a pain or an indigestion. It worried him if he fell off his horse at a joust, if there was an attack of sweating sickness at the palace, if the oysters were bad and gave everyone food poisoning. It worried his ministers and his diplomats. And it worried the ordinary men and women, who worked in the shops, or the mills, or the fields because they liked to feel safe and if their king died, who would protect them then?

Henry and Katherine were not childless. Every now and then a prince or more princesses were born, weak little wheezing things that were greeted with trumpets, swathed in velvet and cloth of gold and laid in jewelled cribs in the Royal Nursery. But they died. The girls died and so did the longed-for boy – baby after baby – except for one, a little girl, whose name was Mary. She survived and she was the darling of both her parents but she was not a boy.

**

This is what Anne came home to find – this little country that was waiting for her. She was 21. She had been away for so long she had a French accent. She had exchanged the glittering courts of Europe for the winter wastes of Norfolk. What did she think? What did she feel when she gazed out of the windows of Blickling, or wandered its childhood corridors in her foreign dresses?

Thomas Boleyn looked at his daughter and saw her difference, her secretive looks. The wedding to Ormonde was not for a while, he thought – why not send her to the English Court? She could join Katherine of Aragon's ladies-in-waiting. It couldn't do any harm. Besides, there was to be a pageant for the Spaniards. Anne could dance couldn't she? She could play Perseverance.

Anne went to London. She acted her part in the pageant. She wore a mask and she danced with the English King. And when she danced, the Court was bound in a spell. Who was this French lady everyone wanted to know? The men were like moths to a light. Have you noticed her grace, her cool wit, her style? She is so private, so difficult to impress. Take off your mask, lady.

So the lady lowered her mask and Henry the Eighth looked, with all the rest. Nothing was the same for him ever again.

**

What did Henry see when Anne Boleyn's mask was lowered? He saw one of his wife's ladies in waiting, a young woman with the most startling cascade of black hair, a look in her dark eyes of challenge and intelligence, a pale face, a long neck and a grace in dancing that completely entranced him.

Or that is one story. How do you know what someone looked like before photographs existed to tell you? There are very few portraits of Anne and they all look different. Which one do you trust? There are descriptions left by people who knew her or met her but even these do not agree. These are some of the things they say: She was slender and graceful. She was shrewish and too tall. She had extremely beautiful hair and a pale face. Her complexion was yellow. She was seductive. She was a

16

witch. She was wise and religious. She had six fingers on one hand. She had a wart on her chin, a beautiful mouth, a growth on her neck that she tried to hide with high-collared dresses. She had a tooth that stuck out over her bottom lip. She was a temptress. The whole court was in love with her. Impossible.

Why was Anne so difficult to describe? Why were some of the reports so vicious? Because people were troubled by her, fascinated by her, afraid of her, jealous of her, or trying to please her. Because she was different. The fact is that people do not bother to spread rumours about someone who is not interesting, and from the range of things said about Anne Boleyn it is clear that she was more than interesting. She was extraordinary.

Perhaps Anne could do better than the Irish Earl. Thomas Boleyn decided to wait and see.

***

But Anne had her own ideas. She had met a man who was young and headstrong. His name was

Henry Percy. He had come to Court in the retinue of Henry's favourite adviser, Cardinal Wolsey, and while his master and the King discussed affairs of state, Percy had got into the habit of visiting the Queen and her ladies. So much more fun, and who was the dark girl sitting quiet in the corner? – the one with the haughty looks?

Before long Percy had whispered will you marry me and Anne had answered yes. Silly fools. Why should they think they would be allowed to marry just because he loved her and she loved him? This was the Tudor court after all. Anne belonged to her father and no one had asked his permission. No one had asked the permission of Percy's father, either.

But worse still, Anne had caught the eye of the King, Henry the Eighth, and since every one of his subjects belonged to him, his permission would have to be sought too.

The King ordered his adviser, Cardinal Wolsey to stop the marriage. NOW. Wolsey shut himself in the long Gallery at York Place – sat at the far end, terrifying in his scarlet robes, with his quiet insults and his smooth grey face. Bring me Percy. Make him walk up the gallery to me. I'll wither him.

'I marvel not a little at thy peevish folly,' Wolsey said softly, when Percy stood before him, 'that thou wouldest tangle and ensure thyself with a foolish girl yonder in the court. I mean Anne Boleyn.'

Why had Percy not asked his father or the King, before he had gone so far, Wolsey wanted to know. Now the King was raging and Percy's father was already on his way, hurrying to court to punish his son.

Percy begged. He pleaded. He crumpled and gave up. And Anne? Anne went back to her duties, with an icy hatred of Wolsey hidden in her heart. To her friends she vowed, 'If it ever lay in her power, she would work the cardinal (Wolsey) as much displeasure.'

Anyone might say as much, after a disappointment – 'I'll give him a taste of his own medicine if I ever get the chance' – only the word Anne uses is not 'chance', a lucky moment that arrives out of the blue, but 'power'. And power was everything in Tudor times. It was life and death, make or break, money, influence, off with his head. She didn't want sad little Percy anymore. She wanted to be able to punish a man as important as the King's favourite counsellor.

Anne was ambitious and Anne was angry, though no one would have noticed. If you passed her any day in the Queen's apartments she bent her head over her needlework. She sat quiet like a good girl. She seemed sensible and willing. But that was only the outside. Inside Anne there was an eagle biding its time, cramping its wings and folding its talons and waiting. Power was what the eagle wanted and there was only one person who had that.

In the prison of her heart, Anne's eagle crouched, and watched the King with its yellow, unblinking eye and set its trap and waited.

***

It took a very long time. The King was smitten with Anne, there was no question about that. He had seen her dancing and he had noticed her long black hair. But when he told Anne of his love she would have none of it. She could not return the love of a man unless he was prepared to marry her. That would ruin her reputation. The King was already married, of course, so it was unfair of him to press her.

He was married, but was he happy? – No, he was not. Did Katherine not understand him? No, she did not. Did she not help with his problems? No. Did he have any problem in particular that troubled him? Yes he did.

He had a serious problem – he had no son to become king after him.

But Katherine could give him a son couldn't she? No, she was too old. Well he must pray to God to send a miracle. God would help – unless, that is, God was cross with him for something – unless God did not like his marriage.

Could that be possible? Could God be punishing him? Had Henry done anything wrong in marrying Katherine, the widowed bride of his elder brother? Surely not.

These were the things that Anne taught Henry to think. These were the ideas that gently with all her softness and all her teasing ways, she fed into him drip by drip and watched him sup them up, like medicine, and waited for them to take effect.

They did take effect. Nothing was lost on Henry, and the more Anne said, the tighter he was bound to her. He needed her youth and her cleverness and her love and his need was like a dragon that grew and burned and threatened to swallow him whole. Anne was not just his beloved, she was the solution to his problem. She would give him a son, if only he could get free of his marriage. She would make his reign secure and happy. He would be able to sleep at night. England would be strong.

***

Anne was never out of Henry's mind. When he left London to go hunting he sent her presents of the deer that he had killed. When he came home again, he took every chance he could find to talk alone with Anne, to ask her what she felt, if she had changed her mind about him. Even in church, Henry passed her notes in his prayer book, begging her for her favour. Was he deceived? Was Anne his?

And Anne would soothe him. Everything was alright.

But it was not long before Henry was anxious again. What did she mean? What did she feel? He wrote to her, late at night, desperate letters. He was 'in great distress'. He did not know what to think. He was in agony – 'struck with the dart of love'.

Anne watched Henry and she caught the infection. It was very exciting to have a king at her feet, and what a king he was – a king who was passionate and hot-tempered, a king who punished people with death and thought nothing of it, a king who was dangerous. Anne was thrilled. She loved him back. Whispering to each other as she worked away in his wife's apartments, they agreed they would marry as soon as Henry had managed a divorce.

At first no one noticed. It was quite normal for the king to have flirtations with younger women. Anne was glamorous and newly arrived from France, what could you expect? She was another of the King's passing fancies. But at the Easter joust, the King entered the lists to fight, in golden armour of a strange new design. On his shield there was a picture of a man's heart squeezed in a press and surrounded by flames. Underneath the heart were the words, 'Declare I dare not.'

Pictures on crests and shields were a language and everyone would have known what his shield was saying. It was as if Henry had ridden out and shouted through a trumpet at the audience, 'I AM BURNING WITH A SECRET LOVE.'

Who was it? Who did Henry love? Buzz buzz went the whisper round the stands as they watched the King couch his lance and gallop at his challenger. Percy knew and so did Wolsey, and Katherine, poor, lonely, Spanish Katherine, who had adored her young husband, she had heard the whispers in her chamber; she knew who the girl was.

Slowly Anne's position at court changed. Henry spent money on velvet and fur for her dresses. He showered her with jewels, rings, bracelets, diamonds for headdresses, diamonds set in true-love knots, diamonds and rubies set in roses and hearts. Anne was no longer the composed, Frenchified, lady-in-waiting. She looked and spoke like a princess. Now people who wanted something from the King came to her for help. She was important. She had power.

She was also impatient. What about this divorce? When and how would it be managed? Henry thought of nothing else. He called it his 'Great Matter'. He explained to Cardinal Wolsey how things stood. Katherine had failed to produce a son and this was because God was angry. It was a punishment. If Wolsey looked in the Bible he would find, in the Book of Leviticus, the sentence, 'And if a man shall take his brother's wife, it is an unclean thing.' Those who do so, 'shall be childless'.

In marrying Katherine, Henry had married the widowed bride of his elder brother. Therefore the marriage to Katherine was unholy. It was an abomination in the eyes of God. Quickly it must be put right and a clean, good, blessed marriage be put in its place.

Henry ordered an official examination into the Royal marriage to be carried out in secret. Wolsey, his trusted friend, his 'wonder wit' was to be in charge. It was all so simple.

Unfortunately, there was one person who had more power than Henry, and that person was the Pope. The Pope was God's representative on earth. Only he could judge what God approved or disapproved. Only he could say whether a marriage was right or wrong. Whatever Henry found in the Bible, whatever he thought or wanted, if the Pope did not agree there would be no divorce.

CHAPTER THREE

How do you keep a secret from a queen? Not all the courtiers thought Anne was a good thing. Many didn't like her. She was getting hoity-toity now that she was sure of the King. She had a sharp and cruel tongue. Many felt loyalty to Katherine, so long-suffering and so ill-used. So it was no surprise that a Chinese whisper went round the court. Henry has ordered a commission to look into divorce. Henry has ordered a divorce. Henry's divorced. Divorce. Divorce. Divorce. Round and round it circled like a deadly little breeze. When it reached the Spanish ambassador, Don Inigo de Mendoza, he stroked his beard and narrowed his eyes and tiptoed to the Queen.

The twirl of Mendoza's hand, like a bird in flight, as he swept Katherine a bow; the oily black of his bent head, his little glittering eyes as he lisped his message, 'Your Majesty, it has come to my ears...'

All the fears that Katherine had tried to stifle, all the rumours she had stopped her ears against rose in her throat and choked her. What could she do if the King were to cast her off? Where would she go? Who would befriend her in this rainy, mud-clogged country she had tried to make her home? A messenger must be sent to Spain to tell her nephew, the Emperor, Charles the Fifth.

Quick, fetch Francisco Felipez. He is a loyal servant. He shall go. A letter was written. Charles would see at once. Katherine was royal, not just English royal, but an Aragonese princess. It was an insult to the kings of Spain. It was outrageous that she could be thrown aside like a holed slipper, no use now that she was too old for childbirth – outrageous to pretend that her marriage to Henry was unholy.

A shaking rage took Katherine. Charles could

fight Henry, she told herself. Spain was so strong. It could reach out its iron arm. It could smash rainy little England, crush this court like an orange under its foot, and paddle in the mess of its juices. It could make a pulp of Henry and his woman.

***

Some snivelling spy saw Felipez hurry out of the palace under cover of darkness. Where was he going without saying goodbye – and what were those packages heavy with sealing wax that he clutched to his chest as he slipped through the shadows? Letters? Oh ho!

So a shifty-faced, slit-eyed cut-throat with a long cold dagger in his hand was sent hurrying down to the docks to catch him. In the inns across France and on the sun-baked plains of Spain he asked for Felipez, followed him like a shadow, waiting for the moment when he would be alone, to slit him and spill his entrails, to burn those letters for Charles the Fifth. But Felipez was going home. Nothing could hold him. He went like a man falling

– back to his own King – and the letters were delivered safely.

**

But politics is a heartless business and though Charles was worried, it did not suit him to fight England yet – soon, but not just yet. But he warned the Pope and the Pope was not impressed.

Henry went to bully Wolsey. Come on Wonder Wit. The divorce. Why was it all so slow? What year were we in now? – 1528. Six years of waiting already, no wonder Henry itched with frustration. No wonder he and Anne were not careful anymore but paraded their love in front of the court, in front of Katherine and her silent Spaniards, even in front of the ordinary people.

For Anne had been seen, on a journey from Windsor Castle, riding pillion with her King, sitting up behind him on the same saddle. The people did not like it. They did not like to see Henry with his arm about another woman's waist and they made their feelings known. Now when Henry was out hunting, labourers in the fields shouted out, 'Back to your wife.'

***

At last Wolsey produced some good news. The Pope was sending a messenger, Cardinal Campeggio, to discuss the divorce.

Anne went home to her father at Hever Castle, and Henry made a speech to the people of London. He chose Bridewell Palace, in the cold of November, and his most sumptuous robes of state. He boomed, at his subjects, legs apart, the picture of an honest king.

If the Pope was to decide, he lied, 'that the Queen is my lawful wife nothing will be more pleasant to me... She is a woman of most gentleness, humility and buxomness... She is without comparison. So that if I were to marry again, I would choose her above all women. But if... our marriage is against God's law, then I shall sorrow, parting from so good a lady and loving companion.'

Then, in case he hadn't made himself plain, he

offered to cut off the head of anyone who disagreed.

No one was fooled, particularly since the divorce talks went badly and Henry found he could not cope without Anne. She was sent for, and soon Campeggio was writing to the Pope that he had seen Henry 'kissing her and treating her as his wife.' This only made the Pope more determined. No divorce – or at least, no divorce yet.

Another envoy was sent to England. A Papal court must be held to look into the problem. The trial was scheduled for the 31st May 1529, but the preparations were so lavish that it had to be put off until the 18th June. If Henry was to go to court like a commoner then it would be no common court. It would be held in the Parliament chamber of Blackfriars and there would be a bridge specially made joining Bridewell Palace to the courtroom so that Henry could make a dignified entrance. Tapestries must be ordered, to ornament this new bridge, and quantities of cloth of gold.

At last all was ready. The Pope's men, in flowing scarlet robes, sat at one end of the Hall on a specially made platform. Their chairs were upholstered in gold cloth and surrounded by railings. The King and Queen sat facing each other on opposite sides of the court on thrones shaded by canopies of gold brocade, (the Queen's throne a little lower than the King's). In the middle of the court were the spectators.

A crier stood to silence the crowd and called out, 'King Harry of England, come into the court.' Henry answered, 'Here, my lords'. He explained his doubts to the scarlet legates, and he insisted that, if his marriage was found lawful he would live happily with Katherine until he died.

Then the crier called, 'Katherine, Queen of England, come into the court.' Katherine made no answer. Small and stony she sat on her golden throne. The crier called a second time. Still – no answer.

So alone in this English court.

No one in all this crowd of thousands, no one to help her – no one to trust. And across the room on his higher throne her lying husband; his mouth stuffed with false promises and his head stuffed with Anne Boleyn. Was there any point in saying anything? Would anything be changed? Slowly Katherine rose to her feet. She was dressed in crimson velvet, trimmed with sable, her skirt slashed to show a yellow brocade petticoat. Splendid and silent she made her way through the press of spectators.

Move back. Move back. It's the Queen. Make way for her Majesty. People shuffled aside, made cramped bows. Round the benches, between the crowded tables, she squeezed her way, her robes crushed, brushing her subjects' legs, sweeping their shoes. At her husband's throne Katherine threw herself on her knees.

She was noble, this Queen that Henry had finished with, and he could not deny it. He raised her to her feet. Again she knelt before him. Again he raised her up. Damn her. Get up woman. She was so noble. It was spoiling his argument. The people were on her side. Henry could feel it in his throat. He would vomit his revenge on these fools. Look at ME. I AM KING.

But now Katherine was speaking. Slowly, in

her deep voice, thick with Spanish accent, she was talking to the husband she loved. Listen.

'Alas Sir, where have I offended you? Or what occasion have you of displeasure, that you intend to put me from you?... I have been to you a true, humble and obedient wife, ever comfortable to your will and pleasure... I never grudged a word or countenance, or showed a spark of discontent...'

Katherine spoke at length. She pointed out that when they married, it had been on the advice of the wise King Ferdinand of Spain, her father, and of Henry's own father, the King of England. They could not have been wrong. She reminded him of the unfairness of the court, where even her own advisors were English subjects. If they spoke for Katherine against his wishes they would be punished. How was this a fair trial? And she asked him to spare her the humiliation of being questioned like a criminal. She would not come to court again.

While she spoke, Henry stared past her, with his brains boiling. When she finished, she rose up from her knees, and leaning on the arm of her gentleman usher she moved slowly out of the court. The people were hushed in admiration. Three times the crier called after her, and Katherine did not so much as turn round. The usher, nervous that she did not answer, said to her, 'Madam, ye be called again.' Katherine answered boldly, so her people could hear,

'It matters not. This is no indifferent court for me. I will not tarry.'

Outside Blackfriars, the Queen was met by hordes of women, who cheered her, blessed her, wept their encouragements.

**

Henry struggled to assert himself. He stood and proclaimed Katherine to be as 'comfortable a wife as I could in my fantasy wish or desire.' Oh yes? The court was hostile. In and out of his lies, Henry flapped like a landed fish. It wasn't for himself he was doing this. It was for the country... for the clergy... for God. It was all a mistake, he was so happy with Katherine. Then he produced a parchment which he said was made out by the bishops of England demanding proof that his marriage was legal – What could he do? Look at the names. They had all signed it – every single one.

NO! They had not all signed it. It was a lie.

What was this? Who said no? Who contradicted the King?

A chaos of whispering took the court. Necks craned. People swivelled, stood on tip-toe. On the bishops' bench one pale man was standing and in his eyes his conscience was alight. Bishop Fisher loved God. He could not lie.

'I did not sign it.'

'Is this not your hand and seal?' asked the King, pretending surprise.

'NO SIRE.'

'Well, well, it shall make no matter. You are but one man.' The King swatted Bishop Fisher's indignation away as though it were a troublesome fly.

But it did matter – because if Fisher's name was on the paper, and if he had not signed it, then it had to be a forgery. And forging the names of bishops is not something that good kings do. It was bad. It was very bad. There was not much chance that Henry was going to get what he wanted out of this court. He knew that now, although the court went on sitting right through the summer and into the autumn. What was worse – he had to go and explain it all to Anne.

⁎

Anne was livid. Henry was a fool – but it was no use punishing him. Someone else must be to blame. Whose fault was it that everything had gone so wrong? Who had made this mess? Inside Anne the eagle raged in its prison. It was hungry now and it wanted blood. Whose blood could it have? Whose death would soothe it?

Wolsey's.

Wolsey must go. He was to blame. Anne hated him. They were sworn enemies she and Wolsey and he knew it. Behind Henry's back he described Anne as 'the midnight crow', 'a continual serpentine enemy about the King'. It was a bad thing for a religious man to say about a woman. The serpent was the devil's disguise. That is how Wolsey saw her – as a she-devil. And he was right in a way, or at least right to be afraid of her. She was ruthless and she had almost unlimited power. The King would do anything she asked, and when Wolsey tried to take the King aside, tried to talk to him in the old way, tried to find five minutes to explain his side of the matter, Anne was always there, always listening, always in the way.

Wolsey was trapped. Slowly Anne turned the King's mind against him. Wolsey was useless. He had achieved nothing. He was worse than useless. He did not have the King's interests at heart. He was treacherous. He was in league with the Pope.

Henry did not know what to believe. He had loved his Wonder Wit. He had trusted him and turned to him in everything. Was Anne right? Was he a traitor? Every time Henry saw his old friend he weakened. Then Wolsey would go and Anne would talk Henry round and the worm of doubt woke up in his brain again.

Towards the end of September the King and Anne were hunting in Northamptonshire, staying in the

King's hunting lodge at Grafton. Campeggio, the Pope's legate was returning home, now that the court hearing was over, and planned to travel down to Grafton to take leave of the King before returning to Rome. He asked if he could bring Wolsey. Yes he could, but there was nowhere for Wolsey to stay. Grafton was very small. A room could be found for Campeggio but Wolsey would have to stay three miles away at Easton Neston.

Here was a state of affairs – Wolsey, the King's old favourite, standing out in the courtyard, denied a room in the house, waiting to be called into the royal presence, with the dust and filth of his journey caked on his clothes. No drink to refresh him, no water to wash the worst of the grime off his face, not even a chair to rest himself in before seeing the King. While he waited like this, Henry Norris, the groom of the stool caught sight of him standing like a servant outside and rushed down to offer him the use of his own room. At least he could change his clothes and refresh himself. As he did so, his last friends and supporters stole into the room in secret, to greet him and tell him the news. Things are bad for you Wolsey. Your time is up. The King has turned against you. Anne has him wound round and round her finger. Good luck. God bless you.

In the packed presence chamber Henry found Wolsey and raised him up from his knees. This man was his friend surely. The old magic began to work again. Henry drew him quietly into a window recess and the two men talked long and earnestly.

What is happening? What is he saying? Did you see the King raise him up with both hands? Yes and he made him put his hat back on his head. That is a rare sign of favour. Wolsey must be back in good grace again. What a miracle.

Anne and her supporters looked black. Old snake face wonder wit pouring his clever words into the King's ear. How could they break his spell? How could they get him apart from the King, for ever? Anne wasted no time. At supper alone with the King she put on her sweetest voice. Wasn't it amazing that the Cardinal could do Henry so much damage and Henry went on forgiving him?

'How so sweetheart?'

Well, goodness, the debt, the slander, the treachery, the dishonour – if it were anyone but Wolsey who had done it, their head would have been cut off long ago. Indeed, it was a miracle that Wolsey's head was still on his shoulders. Cutting off his head was almost no punishment considering the harm he had done, but no doubt Henry knew best. No doubt Henry thought he was safe. No doubt it didn't matter that Wolsey went on getting richer and richer, that he had more and more palaces, more and more power. Perhaps it would be no bad thing if Wolsey were to run the country completely. No... it was true... Henry was very wise not to cut off his head...

After dinner Henry talked with Wolsey again until bed time. But in the morning Anne went to work once more. What was the plan for the day? Henry was to meet Wolsey and have a further conference. They were friends again, didn't Anne know? Wolsey was riding over from Easton Neston even now.

But it was such a lovely day. Wouldn't the King rather ride out with his lady than sit in a dusty room and talk? Sweet Lord, to please me?

When Wolsey dismounted at Grafton Regis with his head full of the happy meetings of the day before, he found the plans had been changed. The King was going riding and staying out for a picnic dinner. He would not be back until after everyone had left. Henry waved a friendly farewell and clattered out of the courtyard.

He never saw Wolsey again.

In October Wolsey was stripped of his office, had all his palaces except one confiscated, and was charged, tried and found guilty. On his way to imprisonment, Henry pardoned him and allowed him to go home, but Wolsey was a broken man. In his bed at Esher, he lay sickening with his dying illness. Henry sent down his own doctor to attend him and Anne sent a jewel off her girdle and pretended messages of love and sympathy. She did so hope he would recover.

A year later, on his way to be tried a second time, Wolsey died. The Boleyns gave a huge banquet to celebrate his death, at which there was a pageant showing Wolsey's descent into Hell.

CHAPTER FOUR

So this is how things stood at Christmas in 1530. Wolsey, the maker and breaker of men, the butcher's son, born in the stinking back alleys of London, who grew up to own four palaces besides Hampton Court, had been broken and was dead. Katherine the forgotten Queen was still living not just with the King, but under the same roof as Anne. And Anne, whom the King kissed openly, and treated as his wife, had her own suite of rooms, her own ladies-in-waiting and walked about the palace as though she owned it. The Boleyns were everywhere at Court – Anne's father, her brother, her uncles, her cousins – all in positions of power, all with unlimited access to the King. But one thing had not

44

changed in all this time, and that was the Pope's mind. He was still not prepared to offer Henry a divorce, and when a huge petition was got together signed by all the English nobility, his response was to order that Anne be dismissed from Court.

Dismissed from Court? It was an outrageous suggestion. For Anne, this meant war. If the Pope thought she could be banished, if he was not prepared to help, he would find that things could go on perfectly well without him. In the meantime, let the English clergy beware. Anne did not like priests and she was on the warpath. When a young clergyman was caught coining money, she had him publicly hanged, in his clerical robes, cut down from the gallows before he was dead, and his intestines pulled out of his stomach while he was alive. Even her father thought it was too much and begged that she let him off. Anne's reply was that there were too many priests in the country already.

Now Anne had an idea. In her time at the Habsburg court she had learnt about the religious free-thinkers, many of whom were living and working on the Continent. These were men who thought that kings were chosen by God, that they were divinely appointed and therefore that there should be no one between a king and God, that a ruler should not ask a priest before he made a decision but pray to God and consult his own conscience.

In England the free-thinkers' books were banned, but they had been being smuggled in illegally ever since 1526. Through her foreign contacts Anne got hold of one and marked the passages that she thought Henry should read with her thumbnail.

Henry was very interested. No one to tell him what he could and couldn't do? No Pope? No appearing at courts of law to answer questions like a commoner, no begging on bended knee? Just to thunder out an order as if from God – to be God's representative, God himself, after a fashion. FANTASTIC.

In February 1531 Henry declared himself head of the Church in England. The Pope threatened to excommunicate him (exclude him from Church) but Henry was not impressed. The Pope was nothing to him now Anne had opened his eyes – just an old man in a silly hat, somewhere across the sea.

'I care not a fig for his excommunications,' Henry said.

For many people this latest trick of Henry's was so wicked it was frightening. The Pope was a descendant of St Peter's, Christ's own apostle. He was the most holy thing imaginable, the closest thing to God himself. To deny him was an insult, a devilish snub, to God, and it would surely be punished.

How many people said what they felt? Only Bishop Fisher, the pale man who had spoken for Katherine at the Papal court in 1529. Usually Henry would not have tolerated criticism, but he was so drunk with this new power he did not mind – indeed he was generous. Someone had tried to poison Fisher. A deadly powder had been sprinkled into the soup but since Fisher was in the habit of sharing his supper with the beggars at his gate it was the beggars who died and not the bishop.

Who had organised this unholy murder? – It was the Boleyns of course, or that is what people said.

Henry thought he had better be seen to disapprove in case it looked like he was involved, so he ordered that the cook be punished. Bravo. What punishment would be fitting? Death obviously. What sort of death? He was to be fried – how else do you kill a cook? – cooked to death in boiling oil.

***

It was all over for Katherine. There was no stopping Anne now. In July, when the Court was staying at Windsor, the King set off on a royal tour taking his mistress. Before he went, he wrote to Katherine telling her not to follow. Katherine wrote back saying that she loved him. She said she had not realised he was leaving – he had not told her – and so she had not been able to say goodbye.

Turning round in his saddle in a rage, Henry shouted at the servant who brought him the letter, 'Tell the Queen that I do not want any of her goodbyes.'

Those were the last words he spoke to his wife of over 20 years. He rode away and he never saw Katherine again. When the Court returned, Katherine was not among the Household. She was sent to one of Wolsey's old palaces, the More, at Rickmansworth, while Anne, still unmarried, took her place at Henry's side. Almost immediately Katherine fell ill. Doctors arrived. They stuck leeches to her body, bled her into buckets, gave her purges that they hoped would make her vomit up her illness.

But Henry didn't care. The next thing on his list of important tasks was to make sure that Anne was grand enough to marry a king. She needed a title, preferably a really monumental title. Lady, duchess, marchioness? Henry wanted something no one had been given before. What could he offer her more than these? – Only earl, duke or marquis, but these were for men.

Wait a minute.

Now that would be something new. It was perfect. She would be the Marquis of Pembroke, the only woman ever to receive a man's honour. At Windsor Castle, before the assembled Court, there was a special ceremony. Anne made her entrance in

49

a robe of crimson ermine, trimmed with velvet and dripping with jewels, her hair perfumed and loose over her shoulders. Kneeling at her lover's feet, Anne received the gold coronet of a Marquis.

Now everything was ready. There was nothing more to be done – except the formality of divorce and marriage. (Henry was not particularly fussed about which order they happened in.) But first Henry would take Anne to Calais and show her off to the King of France.

She must look sensational. What would impress the French? What would dazzle their greedy eyes? The English royal jewels – 20 rubies and two great diamonds – they would do the trick. A messenger was sent galloping to Rickmansworth. Would Katherine kindly give back the Queen's jewellery. Her old lady-in-waiting needed it.

Poor Katherine, on her sick-bed – give up the sacred jewels in which she had been married? Hand them over to a strumpet, a little French trollop, a grabber of husbands? Those jewels had been worn only by crowned Queens. They weren't baubles to be dangled round the neck of any commoner who took the King's fancy. NO SHE WOULD NOT. Had the King gone mad?

The messenger returned out of breath and the whole palace heard the King's response. Won't give them up? Alright... Tell her, I ORDER IT. So the rubies arrived and were stowed among the royal baggage and the long cavalcade wound its way down the lanes to Dover. On 11th October, before dawn, Anne and Henry boarded the *Swallow* and set sail for France.

***

The visit to France was a success. There were jousts and masked pageants and a candle-lit banquet of a 170 different dishes. Most of the Court returned to England on 29th October – or tried to return. The golden weather that had lasted through all the celebrations turned foul. A gale sprang up and tore through the crooked streets of Calais. Those ships which had set out were driven back to shore, or driven on to Flanders. Anne and Henry stayed put. Their lodgings at Calais were so comfortable. They had a King's garden and a Queen's garden, a tennis court, and a gallery to walk in. Anne had a suite of seven main rooms and her bedroom backed on to Henry's own, with interconnecting doors. Why hurry home?

On the 12th November, at midnight, Anne and Henry finally boarded their ship. It was dark winter weather, gales and fog. Like a shuttlecock, the sea and the wind spun the boat between themselves, sometimes forwards, sometimes back. England began to worry. Where was the King? Lost? Wrecked? No news. No sign of a sail. Just the whipping wind and the waves, a world of rain and racing water.

Then a mast – a tiny ship battling home. Two days to make a three-hour crossing. But he's safe. The King is safe. England breathed a sigh of relief. Bells were rung and a thanksgiving sung in St Paul's Cathedral.

***

A month after their return, just before Christmas,

Anne discovered that she was pregnant.

Thank God. A son at last (because it couldn't be a girl, could it?). Now she must be married and crowned Queen. In secrecy, before dawn, Henry and Anne met in a room above the Holbein Gate of Anne's palace, York Place. It was the 25th of January. Where are the witnesses? A whisper from the dark behind – Here Sire. Here's Henry Norris, your trusted friend and Thomas Heneage of the Privy Chamber.

Good. Hurry, before the light comes up, before the public are abroad in the streets.

The priest performing the ceremony asks Henry a question, 'I trust you have the Pope's licence.' Not even Henry could tell a direct lie, 'What else?' But the priest was persistent. Could Henry read out the Pope's permission? Wasn't it annoying but the King had left it in his chamber among his private papers. There was not time to get it now – 'if I should, now that it waxeth towards day, fetch it, and be seen so early abroad, there would rise a rumour… Go forth in God's name and do that which appertaineth to you.'

Get on with it man, in other words. Henry was beginning to lose patience.

So the priest did as he was told. Anne was married at last, and pregnant. And as the first grey light dawned over London, Henry's subjects woke up and shivered into their clothes, unaware that they lived in a country where the King had two wives.

CHAPTER FIVE

Married but not divorced — not so clever. Everywhere there were public protests against Anne. A priest was tried for calling her 'the scandal of Christendom, a whore and a harlot'. The entire congregation of one church walked out in disgust when they were ordered to pray for her. The Dean of Bristol was sacked for forbidding his priests to pray for Henry and Anne, and Margaret Chancellor, an ordinary housewife, was thrown into prison for shouting, 'God save Queen Katherine!' in the street, and for calling Anne 'a goggle-eyed whore'.

But Anne was not going to give up now. Unloved, unwelcomed, despised by her future subjects, she nursed her pregnancy and prepared for coronation. It would be on Whitsunday, the first of June, 1533.

On the 23rd May Archbishop Cranmer pronounced Henry and Katherine's marriage to be 'null and absolutely void' and 'contrary to divine law'. On the 28th he made a public announcement about Henry's marriage to Anne. From a high balcony at Lambeth Palace he blessed it and called it holy. Just in time.

On the 29th, the first of the four days of coronation processions began. First, a river pageant – At the front, a boat carrying mechanical monsters, that jerked their limbs and belched out flames and threw blazing fireworks into the sky. Next came 50 great barges, hung with bunting, decorated with gold foil that glistened in the sun and little bells that tinkled in the breeze. On board there were as many musicians as could be packed on the deck, and in between the musicians there were cannons.

The noise, from the musicians and the cannons and the fireworks was so great that at the Tower of London, where Anne was to stay, all the glass in the houses round about was shattered.

Well, if Henry made enough noise and if the pageants were such as had never before been seen, then the ordinary people would be dazzled. They would go home with their ears buzzing and with stars in their eyes. God's laws would be dizzied right out of their heads. And then they would accept Anne.

The next day everyone rested. Along the route to Westminster preparations were still underway. Grit had to be raked over the streets to stop the horses from slipping. In front of the houses, cloth of gold, cloth of tissue, tapestries and scarlet and crimson velvet banners had to be hung, until the streets made one rich corridor from palace to palace.

***

Saturday, 31st of June, 1533.

What is this long and costly snake that winds its way through the streets to Westminster? It is the Queen's procession of course, moving slow and stately in the first summer heat. What are these spots and stripes of velvet and cloth of gold? They are 12 servants of the new French Ambassador, dressed in blue velvet, with blue and yellow sleeves. They have white plumes in their hats and they ride on white horses, two abreast. And next? They are the nine judges riding in scarlet hoods and gowns, and after them come the knights of the bath, the chancellor, the Archbishops, each one finer than the last. That is the head, but what is the eye of the snake? What is this white eye that dazzles at its centre?

That?

That is Queen Anne. She is dressed in the French fashion, in a surcoat of filmy white, a mantle of white cloth of tissue and a coronet of gold. Her black hair glosses loose over her shoulders and down to her waist. She rides in a litter of white satin, carried on the backs of two palfreys clothed to the ground in white damask. Over her head, the barons of the Cinque Ports carry a canopy of cloth of gold, with gilded staves and silver bells.

Behind the Queen the procession snakes on in crimson and cloth of gold, on horse-back and in carriages. It is slow because it must stop to admire the complicated tableaux that have been set up at different points along the route, a small castle on a hill, a tree that bursts into mechanical flower, the Greek gods and goddesses on Mount Olympus.

And are Henry's subjects dazzled? Do they accept Anne?

At Westminster, where the procession came to a halt Henry stood waiting for her. He took his wife lovingly in his arms, 'How liked you the look of the City sweetheart?' Anne's reply was sour. The City was fine enough but its inhabitants had hats that were stuck to their heads and mouths that were dumb. Only ten people had called out, 'God save your Grace!' What was worse, the banners with 'H' and 'A' intertwined in gold thread had been pointed at, 'HA! HA! HA!' The rude citizens had laughed. No, Anne was not in a good mood.

Never mind. No one could stop her being Queen. For the coronation Anne wore robes of purple velvet, furred with ermine. Her dark hair was loose again but ornamented with a net of pearls. And her head was crowned with a gold coronet specially made for her, as the normal crowns were thought too heavy. Above her a glittering golden canopy and before her the sceptre, the rod of ivory and the crown of Edward the Confessor, carried by the Earl of Oxford. But as tradition dictated, her little feet were naked.

It was tradition too, that a King was not allowed to be present at his wife's coronation. So Henry watched through a specially made lattice-work screen behind the stands. He listened as a solemn high mass was sung. He saw Archbishop Cranmer pray over Anne as she knelt before the altar. He saw Anne anointed with the holy oil, saw her stand and cross over to the throne of Edward the Confessor, draped with cloth of gold and raised on a tapestry dais. He saw her sit and be crowned with the ancient crown, and he saw her take the sceptre and the rod of ivory as the symbols of a reigning queen.

It was done. A messenger rode to Ampthill to tell Katherine that England now had one King but two Queens. He found her lying on a pallet 'sore annoyed with a cough' and crippled with a septic foot.

Meanwhile, Anne emerged into the sunlight of a

summer's day, processed past the clock tower in the New Palace Yard, past five stone cisterns running with free wine for the people of London, and entered Westminster Hall, set out for a vast banquet. Two tables stretched the length of the room with newly gilded seats, where 800 diners, already in place, rose to greet Anne as she arrived. Up the hall she passed, to a marble table on a platform at the far end. Only the Archbishop sat with her. Behind her stood the Countess of Oxford and the Countess of Worcester with a cloth that they would hold in front of her when she needed to be sick. Under the table sat two more countesses in case she needed the chamber pot.

Again Henry watched from another secret balcony. The food was carried into the room behind the Duke of Suffolk and Lord William Howard, both of whom were on horse-back, to a trumpet fanfare and the singing of minstrels. There were 28 dishes for the first course, 24 for the second and 30 for the third. At the end there was dessert, fruit, nuts and sweetmeats loaded on to specially made wax ships.

***

Then it was over and there was nothing else to do but wait for the prince to be born – oh and to bully Katherine and her daughter Mary. They were not to call themselves Queen and Princess anymore. Katherine was to be the Princess Dowager and Mary was to be plain Lady. And what were these new uniforms that Katherine's servants were wearing, with 'H' and 'K' intertwined on their chests? Had Katherine not told her servants to stop bowing and curtseying? Had she not told them to walk forwards out of her presence and not backwards as if she were still Queen?

No she hadn't. And no, no, NO, she wouldn't, and nor would Mary. So mother and daughter were separated. They were not allowed to see each other ever again and Mary was not even allowed to write a goodbye letter. She was 17 and very determined. What if she tried to whip up a following – what if she started writing to Spain, or talking to the English loyal to Mary? Anne tried to bribe her to come to Court. Wouldn't she come? It would be so lovely to see her. It wouldn't be so very difficult to call Anne the Queen would it – just a little curtsey now and then – and her father would be so pleased. Didn't she know how hurt he was by Mary's obstinacy? If only she'd be sensible she could have lovely rooms and lots of new dresses. Wouldn't she?

But Mary was Katherine's daughter. She wrote back saying she knew of no Queen of England except her mother, but if 'Madam Boleyn' would give her love to her father she would be much obliged.

How dare she? 'Madam Boleyn'? – QUEEN ANNE. A spitting temper Anne was in. She would poison Mary at a banquet one of these days. She would make her be a servant. She would marry her off to some pauper of a farmer, some 'varlet'. She would hit her, she told her ladies-in-waiting – she would give her a right 'good banging'.

So Mary had lost her mother and got herself a wicked stepmother, and while she was refusing Anne, Katherine was refusing Henry. A handful of courtiers had been sent to Ampthill with a parchment for Katherine to sign accepting her new title. The gentlemen paled as they watched her score through the words 'Princess Dowager'. Five black lines on top of each other, over and over the hated title, with such violence that the quill tore a hole in the parchment.

I......AM......THE.......QUEEN......AND.... THE.....KING'S.....TRUE.....WIFE.

A tear with every word and the pen like a knife.

Katherine was punished by being moved from Ampthill. She was sent to the Fens, to Buckden, a damp and ancient palace with a tower and a view across the wild and deserted marshes. Henry hoped she would be lonely and miserably un-comfortable. But when she arrived the country people ran in a crowd behind her carriage shouting their support, offering her their lives if she needed them.

Katherine spent her days giving food and drink to the poor, wearing a hair shirt and sewing altar cloths for the local churches. Day and night she prayed, kneeling in a small window that looked on to the chapel. And when she left the window to go to bed, the servants would find the sill wet with tears.

***

In August a message came from Anne. Could she please have the triumphal cloth and the christening gown that Katherine had brought with her from Spain when she first came to marry the King of England. It was so much more sumptuous than the English ones. The request was insulting and insane. Even Henry didn't feel like enforcing it, but Anne was not well and was being even more difficult than usual.

It was almost time for the baby to be born. Anne had been healthy so far but now the Court doctors were shaking their heads. They muttered to each other about fears for her life. What's that you're whispering in the corner man? What are you saying? If it's about my wife, you can come here and tell it to me. You'd better make her fit again or it will be the worse for you.

But in private Henry prayed to God. Don't let her

die. Leave me my wife, my precious hard-won wife. Take the child if you must, but leave me her.

Traditionally a Queen spent the six weeks before and after the birth shut away in her rooms with only women to keep her company. In the middle of August the King and Queen went to Greenwich. This was where the baby was to be born. A great bed of state had been built so that she could receive the people she needed to see from a bed rather than the usual throne, and the walls were hung with heavy draught-proof hangings. Dim light; stuffy, tapestry-dust air; the whisper of women's voices; and the worry of the pain and the difficulty to come – how did Anne pass the creeping time? How many times did she lose her temper with her ladies or wish herself a man?

She did not have long to wait. The baby was born quite easily, at three in the afternoon, on the 7th September. Henry had organised a splendid joust to celebrate the arrival of the little prince.

But the baby was a girl.

In her chamber Anne had to send the news of the baby to the outside world. A document was brought in for her to sign. It read, 'It hath pleased the goodness of Almighty God, of his infinite mercy and grace, to send unto us... a prince.'

With a bitter heart Anne picked up her quill, and, before writing her name, scratched in the 'ss' that made prince into princess. Just another princess. A paltry little girl.

CHAPTER SIX

So what was the point of Anne Boleyn now? She had failed hadn't she – this marvellous young wife, so much better than Katherine, who would produce the heir to Henry's throne? Well, it was only a first child. Henry and Anne made a good job of looking pleased and a sumptuous christening was organised. Bonfires were lit across London and there was free wine for all. Meanwhile, the baby Elizabeth was carried from the Great Hall of Greenwich along a carpet of green rushes and down another tunnel of tapestry hangings, to the Church of the Observant Friars. She returned in the autumn evening, escorted by over 500 flaming torches.

Never mind, Anne was soon pregnant again, and

this time it would definitely be a boy. Henry ordered a silver cradle from his goldsmiths, studded with Tudor roses made of precious stones. To go with it there were gold-embroidered covers and cloth-of-gold baby clothes. Then, to stop any idle tongues that might be chattering in his kingdom, Henry produced a new law, in March 1534, known as the Act of Succession. In other words, the rule about who would take the throne after Henry.

It was this law that turned the paltry little girl into one of our greatest queens – Elizabeth I, Gloriana. It said that there could be no king or queen other than the child of Henry and Anne. So, if they only produced girls, one of *them* and not Mary, Katherine's daughter, who had been born first, would be queen. Everyone was required by law to swear allegiance to the Act, and while they were at it to swear that Henry and not the Pope was the head of the church in England. No one liked the laws but most people managed to take the oath. A few, including the brave Bishop Fisher refused. Again and again he was asked. No, he could not. He would not swear against his conscience.

CUT OFF HIS HEAD THEN. So that is what happened, along with Sir Thomas More and the Nun of Kent and one or two others, and the heads were boiled and put on a spike for all to see, until they turned black in the sun.

At the end of July Anne lost her baby. It was born several months too early and already dead. A girl and a stillborn. The woman was no good. Now, if Henry had fallen in love quickly, he fell out of it just as fast. What did Anne have that was so special? There were so many other girls. He could have any of them. He could have all of them if he wanted. He was the King after all.

So a new chapter opens, in which Henry is unfaithful – and anyone will do. There is a woman at a state banquet. There is a pretty girl out riding with her sweetheart that Henry pulls off her horse and takes back to his castle. There are ladies in waiting, several of them, including Anne's own cousin, Madge Shelton, and a little mouse called Jane Seymour – no need to worry about her though, plain Jane, she wouldn't last long.

What did Anne do? She lost the eagle that had

hunched so hungrily inside her and grew instead a terrible serpent of jealousy. Long, long, with eyes the colour of grass, flexing its coils inside her like a bursting cramp. It made Anne sore and it made her suspicious. She threw tantrums like a child. She wanted the girls dismissed from Court. She wanted people killed – the priests who wouldn't swear, Mary and Katherine, it was always their fault. That would solve it. That would make it all better. I am uneasy my lord. Cut their heads off for me. I can't sleep.

1535 had been a bad year – the year of the mouse, who hung on despite her feeble attractions. Whatever Henry did, there Jane seemed to be behind him, so small, so nothing. Oh squeak my lord. Oh nothing my lord. I quite agree my lord. It is as you wish my lord.

WHY DID HENRY LOVE HER?

Anne had hair the colour of the secret dark. She had dangerous, silken, wrap-you-up-and-swallow-you hair, that sheeted down her back to her waist. The mouse had mouse hair. Anne argued and challenged. The mouse agreed. Anne's eyes flashed, come on I dare you. The mouse had eyes on the ground. Oh no my lord, I daren't look up, I might see something.

Anne couldn't understand it. Look at me. LOOK AT ME. I am a dream. I am everything you want. I am irresistible.

Only I'm not. I'm feeling old. I keep losing babies. I think my eyes don't sparkle like they used to. I am worried about everything. I dream about wrinkles on my face. Is that a grey hair there on the side, by my ear? My youth is slipping through my fingers. Let me hold it still. Give me my beauty at least. Give me a boy. Or just give me back my King.

Then in late October Anne was pregnant again. Now, this time, it must be. It was a race against time – this baby against the King's growing love for the mouse. So Anne had something to cling to at least, as she sat lonely in her apartments, trying, like Katherine before her, not to notice the whispers in the corner, the burning glances that Henry shot at the mouse's bent head.

The winter wore on and although Henry enjoyed

himself he worried about Spain. What if Charles decided to avenge his stubborn aunt? Katherine had been moved again, to Kimbolton, where she was treated like a prisoner. Neither she nor Mary would take the oaths of Succession or Supremacy and they must be brought to heel.

But if Spain should hear how Katherine was treated, what then? There was a lot of support for them in England. If Charles arrived with an army, many English would fight on his side.

Henry needn't have worried. Katherine's health was not good and had been getting steadily worse. On Boxing Day she was in such pain she could neither eat nor drink. The news went out that she was dying and Chapuys, Spain's loyal ambassador, set out determined that she should not die without the companionship of one of her own countrymen.

Two days later, Katherine made her will, which Henry was to ignore. Then on the last evening of her life she dictated a letter. The scribe bent over Katherine's mouth to catch the whispered words. The castle silent in the winter dark and the suffering

Queen speaking out her life,

'My lord and dear husband,

I commend me unto you. The hour of my death draweth fast on... You have cast me into many miseries... I do pardon you all, yea, I do wish and dearly pray God that he will also pardon you... Lastly, I vow that mine eyes desire you above all things.'

She must sign the letter. It was not valid unless she signed. Lift her up. Give her the quill. Put it in her hand. My lady, do you hear? Can you sign my lady?

A last time the southern fire lights the dying eyes. In the arms of her ladies, Katherine moves the quill in a slow scrawl. She writes the title that Henry had tried to take away. She writes her unbroken spirit.

***

They cut her open after she died, to find out the cause of her death. Everything looked normal except for her heart, which had a black growth around it and when they washed the heart and cut it in half, it was black as coal inside.

The Queen Katherine is dead my lord. Chapuys's eye glittered with a tear. But Henry did not feel at all like crying. Now Spain wouldn't bother to fight. 'God be praised that we are free from all suspicion of war!' And Anne said, 'Now I am indeed a Queen.'

The King and Queen dressed in joyful yellow, with white feathers in their caps and carried the baby Elizabeth to Mass in a fanfare of trumpets. It was one of the last times they were happy together. On the 24th January, a fortnight later, Henry fell off his horse in the tiltyard at Greenwich and was knocked unconscious for more than two hours. Anne thought he might die. The shock sent her into labour early and the baby was born – dead again, and a boy.

'It is the voice of God. I see now he will grant me no sons.' Henry's displeasure rumbled around the Court.

'What do you mean the voice of God, my lord? It was the shock of your fall. That was what did it –

your fall and me coming into the room two weeks ago and finding that mouse on your knee. My health has been sorely tried. You did it! You killed my child.'

Tantrums did Anne no good. The Seymours were everywhere at Court just as the Boleyns had once been. There was an ill wind blowing and Anne was in its path.

Chapuys was summoned to Court, where Henry instructed him: Tell your master, Charles, that we wish to renew our friendship with Spain. Katherine is dead now; there is no reason for us to stay enemies.

Here, Cromwell, you, Thomas Cromwell, you shall be in charge of it. See that the Emperor Charles makes a treaty with us.

Cromwell scratched his head and cursed his luck. Here was a problem. Charles would make no treaties while Anne was on the throne. But Anne was Cromwell's friend, she had helped him to his present office, she had used her influence on his behalf. He was the new man at court. He was the new Wolsey, but what had happened to Wolsey? He had died on his way to trial and possible execution. What happened to anyone who failed for the King? They ended up on a spike outside the Tower of London, no matter who they were.

It was not a difficult decision. Late in Easter week 1536, Cromwell put his mind to 'think up and plan' the downfall of the Queen.

CHAPTER SEVEN

Quick Anne. You are no fool. Act. Hold up your hand and stop these plotting men. You have so little time. Don't you feel the wind of your death blowing towards you from the other side?

But Anne was frozen. She had felt the wind – she knew it only too well. She had whistled it up so often for other people. She recognised it when it came for her and it chilled her to a stand still.

Cromwell was fast. There was no space, for him, between thought and action. As soon as his brain conceived a plan, his will had put it into practice. On the 29th April he put his story to the King. He had unearthed a plot against the King's life, in which the Queen, and several gentlemen of the Privy

Chamber were involved. Henry's eyes started out of his head. He goggled at the paper. All these people plotting against him? It was terrifying. Arrest them. Arrest them all. There shall be no mercy.

But what about Anne? She was his wife – he couldn't arrest her. Cromwell was soothing. Henry was so good he had not noticed. She was no wife. Why did he think he had no son? It was not Henry's fault. He had been seduced by witchcraft. No man was safe against the power of a witch, not even the greatest King.

A witch? Was Anne Boleyn a witch? My God, of course, and he had never seen it. She had wound him into wedlock with her black arts, her wicked spells. And Katherine had been right. What horror he had suffered. How dangerous it might have been. He must pray at once. He must be saved. Act. Act now.

On 30th April, Mark Smeton, a young Court musician was staying as a guest at Cromwell's house. He awoke to find six men bursting into his chamber.

'Get up. You're under arrest. Treason. Get your

clothes on. Cromwell's orders.'

What had Smeton done? He was amazed. Cromwell told him. He had been part of a wicked ring of witchcraft and adultery. He had been the Queen's lover along with Henry Norris, Francis Weston, William Brereton and Anne's brother George Rochford.

WHAT? Anne and her brother? Lovers? Don't be ridiculous. And Norris was the King's best friend. They were all the King's friends.

Not any more they weren't. Get your clothes on or we'll take you naked.

Smeton panicked. It was all so mad, so nonsensical. Surely no one would believe it. Surely Cromwell was raving. But he was wrong. They would believe it. Cromwell would make sure of that.

They took him to the Tower for questioning. When he denied his crimes he was tortured for 24 hours. They beat him, tied him to the rack and stretched him. They tied a knotted rope round his head, over his eyes, and tightened it till his skull cracked. He gave in. He said everything Cromwell wanted him to say and then he was dragged away and kept in a dungeon with his legs in irons, in case he changed his mind.

Smeton was only the Court musician so no one noticed that he did not appear at the Mayday joust. And while he screamed in the Tower, Rochford and Norris galloped against each other in the lists, completely unaware that Cromwell's net would close about them next. Henry left the joust early and called Norris to ride with him. As they rode, he questioned his old friend. Cromwell had unearthed a plot. Norris was named. Had he done these things? What had he to say for himself? Norris swore his innocence on his life. He had never heard such arrant nonsense. But Cromwell's plan had infected Henry's wits. The word of a friend meant nothing to him any more.

Prove it then. Prove it in the Tower. Arrest this man.

So Norris was taken to the Tower, in the early hours of the 2nd May, where Rochford, Anne's brother was to join him. By the end of the day all the arrests had been made.

And now for Anne. She was sitting at dinner

when they came for her. It was her uncle Norfolk, who told her what she was guilty of. He had fallen out with Anne and was eager for her disgrace. Anne bore herself bravely. If the King wanted her to go to the Tower she would do so with pleasure. Would they wait while she fetched some clothes, while she packed up some things? No, they couldn't wait. She was to come now, as she was.

Down to the river under escort, on to a barge, and the same journey as she had made to her coronation. Usually prisoners were taken to the Tower under cover of darkness but Cromwell made Anne do it in daylight, while all of London stared and pointed. Only when she was inside the yard did she break down, screaming and laughing by turns and falling on her knees at the feet of her accusers.

***

Friday 12th May 1536, Westminster Hall, where Anne's coronation banquet had been held. This time the Hall was bare. No tapestry, no gold, no marble table laden with food, just the timber scaffolding benches of the law court and the executioner, holding his great axe, its blade turned in to the wall. It was the trial of Weston, Norris, Brereton and Smeton. To do the job, Cromwell had assembled a jury of men who hated the defendants or wanted to curry favour with Cromwell – Edward Willoughby who owed money to Brereton and couldn't pay, Walter Hungerford who was paid by Cromwell to do his bidding, William Askew who was a supporter of Katherine's Mary.

The men were tried together, without the chance to speak individually, without hope that one man's case might be different from another's.

Everyone watched the axe. If the defendants were innocent the blade stayed facing the wall. If not...

Flash of cold light as the axe swung into the room. Pointed its cutting steel at the four men. GUILTY. The judgment was traitor's death: half strangulation, disembowelling, castration and the removal of the victims' arms and legs. Take the prisoners back to the Tower.

Anne and her brother were not tried until after the weekend. Special stands had been built, this time in the Great Hall of the Tower, for all the people who would come to watch. There were two thousand spectators. Anne's uncle Norfolk presided over the trial as lord steward under a great cloth of estate. There was a jury of 26 peers as well as the chancellor and the royal justices. Anne was led in first, to be sat in a chair in the middle of the Hall. Raising her right hand she pleaded 'not guilty' to all the charges.

With a quiet voice she answered her accusers:

No she had not been unfaithful to her husband the King.

No she had not promised to marry Norris.

No she had not hoped for the King's death.

No she had not given secret presents and signs to Norris.

No she had not poisoned Katherine.

No she had not planned to poison Mary.

Her tiny head up, looking at the jury with her challenging eye. Even Anne's enemies were shamed into admiration. 'She made so wise and discreet answers… excusing herself with her words so clearly as though she had never been faulty.' At last she had proved herself noble. Not that it did her any good.

Once more the axe blade swung into the room. Her uncle Norfolk pronounced the sentence, weeping as he did so. 'Thou shalt be burnt here within the Tower of London, on the Green, or else to have thy head smitten off, as the King's pleasure shall be…'

Anne accepted her sentence with dignity. She had been proud, she said, 'I admit too, that I have taken it into my head to be jealous of him… But may God be my witness if I have done him any other wrong.' She did not complain. She blamed no one. She just asked for time to make her peace with God.

Then she was gone.

CHAPTER EIGHT

How did Henry want his wife to die – by burning or beheading? Well, he was rid of her now, why not be kind? She could be beheaded and as a special treat she would be spared the axe, which so often made a mess of things. Henry would send to Calais for a French executioner and a sword.

Alone in the Tower, Anne waited for her death. The night before she died she did not sleep. She woke her servants early and ordered a mass. Then she swore on the sacrament that she was innocent and sat down until they came for her. When the constable of the Tower came in to see her she asked about the delay.

'I thought to be dead by this time and past my pain.' Why madam, did she not know? There would be no pain. The constable swiped the air with expertise. The blow was 'so subtle' she would feel nothing.

Anne answered him, 'I heard say the executioner was very good, and I have a little neck.' Then she circled her neck with her hands and burst into laughter.

***

What a crowd is here to see me die.

Out through the Cole Harbour Gate and the scaffold four feet high and draped in black. So many, many people, so many familiar faces. And then the press of commoners come to gawp at blood and then go home and guzzle their bread and beer and go on drawing breath, as though nothing had happened. The thump of her heart in her ears, the prickle on the back of her neck and her mouth dry.

Don't sink in front of them. Bear me up bravely

my legs. One cut and all is over. Courage Queen Anne. Courage.

She wears a mantle of ermine with a hood, over a grey damask gown; a petticoat crimson like blood. Up the scaffold she steps. Now she speaks to the crowd. Her head is up. Her voice calm, 'Good Christian people I have not come here to preach a sermon; I have come here to die... for according to the law and by the law I am judged to die, and therefore I will speak nothing against it. I am come hither to accuse no man... But I pray God save the King and send him long to reign over you, for a gentler nor a more merciful prince was there never, and to me he was ever a good, a gentle and sovereign lord...

'And thus I take my leave of the world and of you all, and I heartily desire you all to pray for me.'

Then, with a 'goodly, smiling countenance', she takes leave of her weeping servants. A lady unfastens her ermine cloak and the long neck is bare. Anne herself takes off her headdress. Silence in the watching crowd. She twists up her famous hair, tucking it into a cap so there is nothing in the way of the sword. Down on the dais she kneels. She is anxious that her head will be cut off before she is ready. She looks over her shoulder continually. One of her ladies puts on the blindfold and Anne holds her hands together in prayer.

'Jesu receive my soul; O Lord God have pity on my soul. Jesu receive my soul; O Lord God have pity on my soul. Jesu receive my s...'

The body crumples. Forward step the weeping ladies and cover it with a cloth. The head too, gathered into a sheet. Red, red soaking through the white. Through the crowd they pass, the ladies, carrying their Queen unhelped to the chapel.

Goodbye sweet lady. Goodbye Anne. Lay her in the box. The body still warm and the blood everywhere.

***

Anne Boleyn was buried in the chapel of St Peter next to her brother George Rochford, three years and 37 days after her coronation.

Anna of the thousand days they call her.

Key dates

1501	Anne is born
1504	Anne's brother George born
1513	Anne goes to Habsburg Court, and spends two years in Flanders and then seven more in France
1520	Field of the Cloth of Gold
1521	Anne returns to England
1522	Anne meets Henry VIII
1527	Henry tells Katherine of Aragon he wants divorce
1529	Divorce proceedings start – a Papal Court is held at Blackfriars
1530	The arrest and death of Wolsey
1531	Henry is made head of the Church
1532	Anne is made Marquis of Pembroke
	Henry and Anne go to France on state visit
1533	Anne and Henry marry
	Anne is crowned Queen
	The birth of Elizabeth I
1536	Katherine of Aragon dies
	Anne is charged with treason and executed

Acknowledgements

Lots of children helped with this book, and I would like to thank them all. They are George Apperly, Serena Coulson, Brilliana Harley, and, from Two Mile Ash Middle School, Milton Keynes: Jack Bartlett, Jason Gibbs, Grace Bright, Anna Chapman, Adam Johnson, Simren Gill, Stephen Miceli, Kayleigh Mcdonald, Andrew Stockbridge, Anne Harriman, Jake Jones and Jenny Dudden.

Author biography

Laura Beatty's biography *Lillie Langtree* is
available in Vintage paperback. She lives in
Northamptonshire and has three children.

OTHER TITLES IN THE **WHO WAS...** SERIES

David Livingstone
The legendary explorer
Amanda Mitchison
1-904095-84-4

Admiral Nelson
The sailor who dared all to win
Sam Llewellyn
1-904095-65-8

Emily Davison
The girl who gave her life for her cause
Claudia FitzHerbert
1-904095-66-6

Sam Johnson
The wonderful word doctor
Andrew Billen
1-904095-77-1

Ada Lovelace
The computer wizard of Victorian England
Lucy Lethbridge
1-904095-76-3

Alexander Selkirk
Survivor on a desert island
Amanda Mitchison
1-904095-79-8

Annie Oakley
Sharpshooter of the Wild West
Lucy Lethbridge
1-904095-60-7

Charlotte Brontë
The girl who turned her life into a book
Kate Hubbard
1-904095-80-1

Ned Kelly
Gangster hero of the Australian outback
Charlie Boxer
1-904095-61-5

William Shakespeare
The mystery of the world's greatest playwright
Rupert Christiansen
1-904095-81-X

HIEROGLYPHIC ALPHABET

A		J		SH	
B		K		T	
C		L		TH	
CH		M		U	
D		N		V	
E		O		W	
F		P		X	
G		Q		Y	
H		R		Z	
I		S			

ALSO AVAILABLE

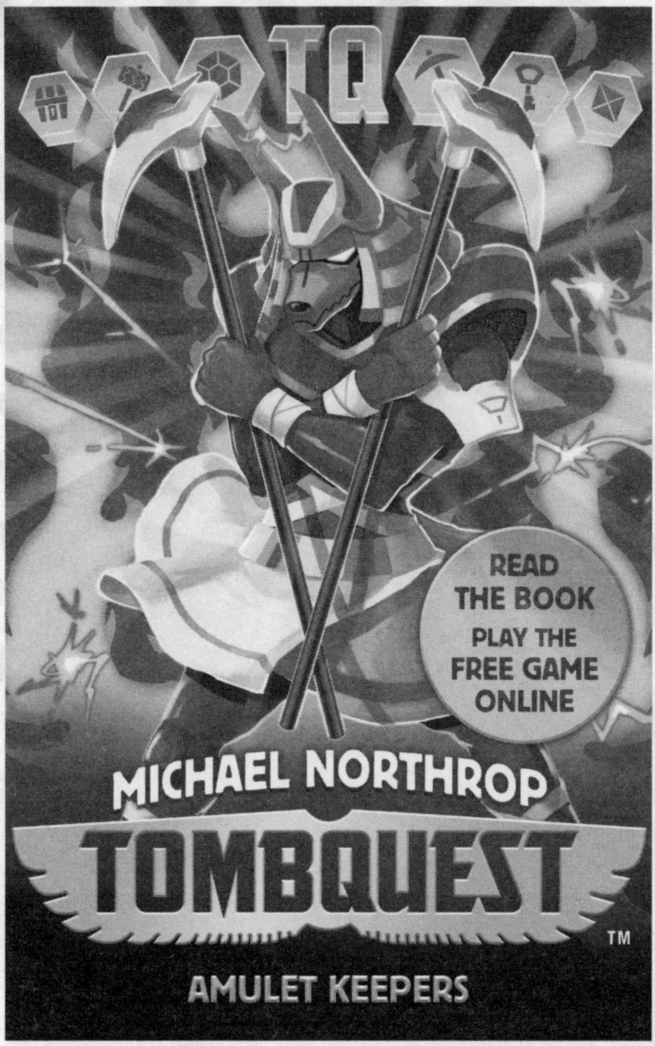